P9-CFO-571

To _____
_____
_____

From _____
_____
_____

Message _____
_____
_____
_____

101 WAYS TO HAVE A HAPPY DAY

CHRISTIAN ART
PUBLISHERS

Published by Christian Art Publishers
PO Box 1599, Vereeniging, 1930, RSA

© 2015
First edition 2015

Cover designed by Christian Art Publishers

Images used under license from Shutterstock.com

Printed in China

ISBN 978-1-4321-1345-2

17 18 19 20 21 22 23 24 25 26 – 12 11 10 9 8 7 6 5 4 3

IN EVERYTHING

GIVE

THANKS!

1 Thessalonians 5:18

01

Find 10 things
to be grateful for
throughout the day.
Praise God for
His blessings!

Do not be anxious about anything,
but in every situation, by prayer
and petition, with thanksgiving,
present your requests to God.
And the peace of God, which
transcends all understanding,
will guard your hearts
and your minds in Christ Jesus.

Philippians 4:6-7 NIV

02

Bake a batch of cookies or muffins. Then make someone's day with a surprise sweet treat.

"It is more blessed to give
than to receive."
Acts 20:35 NLT

Happiness comes when we stop complaining about the troubles we have and offer thanks to God for all the troubles we don't have.

03

Because You are my help, I sing in the shadow of Your wings.

Psalm 63:7 NIV

04

Sing your favorite hymn as you go about your daily chores. Meditate on the words and make it a time to worship and praise God amidst the busyness of the day.

Sing praises to God and to His name!
Sing loud praises to Him
who rides the clouds. His name
is the LORD – rejoice in His presence!
Psalm 68:4 NLT

05

Instead of eating lunch inside,
have a picnic outside.
Food tastes so much better
when mixed with fresh air!

Taste and see that the LORD is good.
Oh, the joys of those
who take refuge in Him!

Psalm 34:8 NLT

06

The secret of being happy
is accepting where you are
in life and making the most
out of every day.

Rejoice in the LORD and be glad.
Psalm 32:11 NIV

Say No to FOMO:
Ban all media for
a day and take
a break from
technology.

07

"Come with Me by yourselves to a
quiet place and get some rest."

Mark 6:31 NIV

08

See
Miracles
In
Life
Every day

Praise the LORD, for the LORD is good;
sing praises to His name,
for it is pleasant.

Psalm 135:3 NKJV

09

Browse around a secondhand
bookstore and restock your
bookshelf with a few
old favorites.

Apply your heart to instruction
and your ears to words of knowledge.

Proverbs 23:12 NKJV

10

Happiness is like jam.
You can't spread even a little
without getting some
on yourself.

Glory in His holy name; let the hearts
of those who seek the Lord rejoice!

Psalm 105:3 ESV

Buy a journal and write down your thoughts, motivational quotes and favorite Scripture verses.

11

Fix your thoughts on what is true,
and honorable, and right, and pure,
and lovely, and admirable.
Think about things that are excellent
and worthy of praise.

Philippians 4:8 NLT

12

Watch the sun set.
Take 30 minutes out
of your day to be still
and to appreciate
the beauty of the
setting sun.

The heavens declare the glory of God;
the skies proclaim the work
of His hands.

Psalm 19:1 NIV

13

Start today with a grateful heart.

Be thankful in all circumstances,
for this is God's will for you
who belong to Christ Jesus.

1 Thessalonians 5:18 NLT

14

66 Don't stay angry.
For every minute you are angry
you lose sixty seconds
of happiness. **99**

Ralph Waldo Emerson

"Don't sin by letting anger control you."
Don't let the sun go down
while you are still angry.

Ephesians 4:26 NLT

Enjoy life's
tiny pleasures:
Watch a bee buzz
or a butterfly flitter
on a flower in the sun.

15

Rejoice in the Lord always.

Philippians 4:4 NKJV

16

Happiness is not having what you want. It is wanting what you have. Choose today to count your blessings.

The LORD bless you and keep you;
the LORD make His face shine upon you,
and be gracious to you; the LORD lift up
His countenance upon you,
and give you peace.

Numbers 6:24-26 NKJV

17

Change your screensaver
on your phone or computer to
something that makes
you laugh or smile.

A joyful heart is good medicine.
Proverbs 17:22 ESV

18

Attitude is everything.
Life is 10% of what happens
to you and 90% of
how you react to it.

In Him our hearts rejoice,
for we trust in His holy name.
Let Your unfailing love surround us,
LORD, for our hope is in You alone.

Psalm 33:21-22 NLT

Go for a walk or a run.
Take it slow and
enjoy the scenery.
Be conscious of each
stride and appreciate
your body for what it is:
a remarkable gift.

19

Do you not know that your bodies are
temples of the Holy Spirit, who is in you,
whom you have received from God?
You are not your own;
you were bought at a price.
Therefore honor God with your bodies.

1 Corinthians 6:19-20 NIV

20 | Celebrate the life you have and not the one you wish you had.

I delight greatly in the LORD;
my soul rejoices in my God.
For He has clothed me with garments
of salvation and arrayed me
in a robe of His righteousness.

Isaiah 61:10 NIV

21

Everybody wants happiness,
nobody wants pain, but you
can't have a rainbow without
a little rain. Realize that tough
times will come, but the sun
will shine again.

Blessed is the one who perseveres under trial
because, having stood the test,
that person will receive the crown of life that
the Lord has promised to those
who love Him.

James 1:12 NIV

22

Plan a weekend away
to somewhere you've
never been before.

Great is the LORD!
He is most worthy of praise!
1 Chronicles 16:25 NLT

"Think of all the beauty
left around you
and be happy."

23

Anne Frank

Happy are the people
whose God is the LORD!

Psalm 144:15 NKJV

24 | Don't dwell on your past mistakes. Learn from them and strive to do better next time.

He said to me, "My grace is sufficient for you, for My power is made perfect in weakness." Therefore I will boast all the more gladly about my weaknesses, so that Christ's power may rest on me.

2 Corinthians 12:9 NIV

25

Five simple rules for happiness:
- Free your heart from hatred
- Free your mind from worries
- Live simply
- Give more
- Expect less

Oh, the joys of those who do not follow the advice of the wicked. But they delight in the law of the LORD. They are like trees planted along the riverbank, bearing fruit each season. Their leaves never wither, and they prosper in all they do.

Psalm 1:1-3 NLT

26

Bloom where you're planted.

Delight yourself in the LORD, and He
will give you the desires of your heart.

Psalm 37:4 ESV

Grab a cup of tea or coffee and enjoy it outside. Enjoy the feel of the sun on your skin and the wind in your hair. Take a few minutes to just BE.

27

Truly my soul finds rest in God;
my salvation comes from Him.

Psalm 62:1 NIV

28

"The best way to
cheer yourself up
is to try to cheer
somebody else up."

Mark Twain

The cheerful heart has a continual feast.
Proverbs 15:15 ESV

29

“Happiness is an inside job.”

William Arthur Ward

Whatever you do,
work at it with all your heart,
as working for the Lord.

Colossians 3:23 NIV

30

Make sure you get enough sleep. Waking up refreshed will give you a spring in your step and a smile on your dial.

In peace I will both lie down and sleep;
for You alone, O LORD,
make me dwell in safety.

Psalm 4:8 ESV

Count your blessings, not your troubles.

31

Blessed is the one who trusts in the Lord, whose confidence is in Him.

Jeremiah 17:7 NIV

32 | Let go and let God.

You bless all of those
who trust You, Lord.

Psalm 40:4 CEV

33

Plant some herbs or vegetable seeds in your garden or in a pot on your veranda. Have fun watching them grow.

For everything there is a season,
a time for every activity under heaven.
A time to be born and a time to die.
A time to plant and a time to harvest.

Ecclesiastes 3:1-2 NLT

34

One of the best feelings in the
world is knowing that someone
is happy because of you.

_____

"In everything, do to others what you
would have them do to you."

Matthew 7:12 NIV

True happiness is giving it away.

35

The generous will prosper;
those who refresh others will
themselves be refreshed.

Proverbs 11:25 NLT

36

If you want happiness for an hour – take a nap.
If you want happiness for a day – go fishing.
If you want happiness for a year – inherit a fortune.
If you want happiness for a lifetime –
help someone else.

Proverb

"Whoever wants to be a leader among you
must be your servant,
and whoever wants to be first among you
must become your slave.
For even the Son of Man came not to
be served but to serve others and to give
His life as a ransom for many."

Matthew 20:26-28 NLT

37

Go star gazing. Take a blanket
and go and lie outside in the
dark. Gaze up at the stars and
see if you can spot a shooting
star. Marvel at the amazing
universe our God created.

When I consider Your heavens, the work
of Your fingers, the moon and the stars,
which You have set in place, what is mankind
that You are mindful of them,
human beings that You care for them?

Psalm 8:3-4 NIV

38

Plant smiles.
Grow laughter.
Harvest love.

Sing of the LORD's great love forever.

Psalm 89:1 NIV

Go through your CD
collection and put
on some music
you haven't listened
to in a long time.
Then take a long,
indulgent bubble bath.

39

You shall have a song as in the night,
and gladness of heart, as when one sets out
to the sound of the flute.

Isaiah 30:29 ESV

40 | Life is beautiful! Enjoy every minute of today!

I will praise the LORD at all times.
I will constantly speak His praises.
I will boast only in the LORD.
Come, let us tell of the LORD's greatness;
let us exalt His name together.

Psalm 34:1-3 NLT

41

Seek joy in what you give, not in what you get.

"Give, and it will be given to you.
A good measure, pressed down,
shaken together and running over."

Luke 6:38 NIV

42

Offer to make dinner for a friend. Ask them about their favorite dish, and deliver it to their home.

"Love one another. As I have loved you,
so you must love one another.
By this everyone will know that you are
My disciples, if you love one another."

John 13:34-35 NIV

Life is like a camera.
Focus on what
is important, capture
the good times,
develop from the
negatives, and if
things don't work out,
take another shot.

43

The LORD has done great things for us,
and we are filled with joy.

Psalm 126:3 NIV

44

When you next
give a gift,
make a card
by hand instead
of buying one.

Beloved, let us love one another,
for love is from God, and whoever loves
has been born of God and knows God.

1 John 4:7 ESV

45

Life is not measured by
the number of breaths we take,
but by the moments that
take our breath away.

We thank You, O God! We give thanks
because You are near.
People everywhere tell
of Your wonderful deeds.

Psalm 75:1 NLT

46

Pick or buy a bunch of flowers
and put them somewhere in your
home where you can see them
and enjoy their fragrance.

Walk in the way of love, just as Christ loved
us and gave Himself up for us as a fragrant
offering and sacrifice to God.

Ephesians 5:2 NIV

Be happy
not because
everything is good,
but because you
can see the good
in everything.

47

May the righteous be glad
and rejoice before God;
may they be happy and joyful.

Psalm 68:3 NIV

48

Always remember
that God is the
source of all true joy
and happiness.
Only in Him can
we be truly happy.

We know that God causes everything
to work together for the good of those
who love God and are called according to
His purpose for them.

Romans 8:28 NLT

49

There are so many beautiful
reasons to be happy.

You have made known to me
the paths of life; You will fill me
with joy in Your presence.

Acts 2:28 NIV

50

Over the weekend,
take a nap in the afternoon –
but make sure it's guilt-free.
Go on, you deserve it!

It is useless for you to work so hard from
early morning until late at night, anxiously
working for food to eat; for God gives rest
to His loved ones.

Psalm 127:2 NLT

Stop giving yourself
reasons why you can't
and start giving
yourself reasons
why you can.

51

Christ gives me the strength
to face anything.

Philippians 4:13 CEV

52

"It isn't what you have, or who you are, or where you are, or what you are doing that makes you happy or unhappy. It is what you think about."

Dale Carnegie

Shout for joy to the LORD, all the earth.
Worship the LORD with gladness;
come before Him with joyful songs.

Psalm 100:1-2 NIV

53

Never put the key to your happiness in someone else's pocket.

Surely God is my salvation;
I will trust and not be afraid.
The Lord, the Lord Himself,
is my strength and my defense;
He has become my salvation.

Isaiah 12:2 NIV

54

Life doesn't have to be perfect
to be wonderful.

Oh come, let us sing to the Lord;
let us make a joyful noise to the rock
of our salvation!

Psalm 95:1 ESV

Let go of what you
think life is supposed
to look like and
celebrate it for
everything it is.

55

May you be filled with joy,
always thanking the Father.

Colossians 1:11-12 NLT

56

Sign up to attend a course at your church that you've not done before.

Wisdom will enter your heart,
and knowledge will fill you with joy.

Proverbs 2:10 NLT

57

Joy doesn't come from
what we get,
but from what we give.

Let us not become weary in doing good,
for at the proper time we will reap
a harvest if we do not give up.
Therefore, as we have opportunity,
let us do good to all people.

Galatians 6:9-10 NIV

58

Choose joy.
“ Joy does not simply
happen to us. We have to
choose joy and keep choosing
it every day. ”

Henri Nouwen

The joy of the LORD is your strength.
Nehemiah 8:10 NKJV

Try something new –
find a recipe that
looks delicious
and that has
ingredients you
haven't tried before.

59

So whether you eat or drink,
or whatever you do,
do it all for the glory of God.

1 Corinthians 10:31 NLT

60

Offer to look after someone's children while they go out on a date with their spouse. Then do something fun with the kids, like baking, drawing or playing a game.

Children, you show love for others
by truly helping them, and not merely
by talking about it.

1 John 3:18 CEV

61

Dance in the rain!
And don't care if anyone
is watching.

Praise His name with dancing,
accompanied by tambourine and harp.
For the LORD delights in His people;
He crowns the humble with victory.

Psalm 149:3-4 NLT

62

" Let us be grateful to
the people who make us happy;
they are the charming gardeners
who make our souls blossom. "

Marcel Proust

Sing to the LORD,
for He has done wonderful things.
Make known His praise around the world.

Isaiah 12:5 NLT

Send a message to an old friend and invite them over for tea and cake.

63

Two people are better off than one,
for they can help each other succeed.
If one person falls, the other can
reach out and help.

Ecclesiastes 4:9-10 NLT

64

"Worry never
robs tomorrow
of its sorrow.
It only saps today
of its joy."

Leo Buscaglia

"Do not be anxious about tomorrow,
for tomorrow will be anxious for itself.
Sufficient for the day is its own trouble."

Matthew 6:34 ESV

65

Choose your favorite fruit
and make an ice cream
or a fruit smoothie.

The fruit of the Spirit is love, joy, peace,
patience, kindness, goodness,
faithfulness, gentleness, self-control.

Galatians 5:22-23 ESV

66

"If you spend your whole life
waiting for the storm,
you'll never enjoy
the sunshine."

Morris West

Let everything that has breath
praise the LORD! Praise the LORD!
Psalm 150:6 NLT

Offer to walk your
elderly neighbor's dog,
or the dog of a friend
who struggles to find
the time to do so.

67

If our faith is strong, we should be patient
with the Lord's followers ... We should try to
please them instead of ourselves.
We should think of their good
and try to help them by doing
what pleases them.

Romans 15:1-2 CEV

68

Indulge in a day of culture: Visit a museum, attend an art exhibition or go to the theater.

They feast on the abundance of Your house, and You give them drink from the river of Your delights.

Psalm 36:8 ESV

69

> " The first recipe
> for happiness is:
> Avoid too lengthy meditation
> on the past. "

André Maurois

Sing the praises of the LORD,
you His faithful people;
praise His holy name.
For His anger lasts only a moment,
but His favor lasts a lifetime;
weeping may stay for the night,
but rejoicing comes in the morning.

Psalm 30:4-5 NIV

70

Make homemade chocolate
sauce for ice cream or
hot chocolate by melting
a chocolate bar and
adding milk or cream.

Whatever you do, whether in word or deed,
do it all in the name of the Lord Jesus,
giving thanks to God the Father.

Colossians 3:17 NIV

Indulge in a childhood
fun activity like
flying a kite,
blowing bubbles
or balloons.
As Winnie the Pooh
says, "Nobody can be
uncheered with
a balloon!"

71

I will sing to the LORD all my life;
I will sing praise to my God as long as I live.
May my meditation be pleasing to Him,
as I rejoice in the LORD.

Psalm 104:33-34 NIV

72

Deal with clutter: spend 20 minutes tidying up your desk – you will feel so much better once it is done!

You thrill me, LORD,
with all You have done for me!
I sing for joy because of what You have done.

Psalm 92:4 NLT

73

"When one door of happiness closes, another opens, but often we look so long at the closed door that we do not see the one that has been opened for us."

Helen Keller

Commit everything you do to the Lord.
Trust Him, and He will help you.

Psalm 37:5 NLT

74

Make small talk with
a stranger – a cashier
or shop assistant –
and take a moment to find out
how they are.

Clothe yourselves with tenderhearted mercy,
kindness, humility, gentleness, and patience.

Colossians 3:12 NLT

"Success is not the key to happiness. Happiness is the key to success. If you love what you are doing, you will be successful."

75

Albert Schweitzer

Commit your works to the LORD,
and your thoughts will be established.

Proverbs 16:3 NKJV

76

Get some vitamin D: Make a conscious effort to spend time outside and catch some feel-good rays!

God's love and kindness will shine upon us like the sun that rises in the sky.

Luke 1:78 CEV

77

Today is a gift from God,
that's why it's called the present.
Live each day to the full
and treat it as a precious gift.

Let all that I am praise the LORD;
with my whole heart,
I will praise His holy name.

Psalm 103:1 NLT

78

Rearrange the furniture in
one room of your house.

Put off your old self ... be made new
in the attitude of your minds.

Ephesians 4:22-23 NIV

When something bad
happens, you have
three choices:
You can either
let it define you,
let it destroy you,
or you can
let it strengthen you.

79

We rejoice in our sufferings, knowing
that suffering produces endurance,
and endurance produces character,
and character produces hope, and hope
does not put us to shame, because God's love
has been poured into our hearts through
the Holy Spirit who has been given to us.

Romans 5:3-5 ESV

80

Eat more fruits and vegetables. Research has shown that eating in a more healthy way has many positive effects, such as better overall health, increased creativity and positive emotions.

God said, "I have provided all kinds of fruit and grain for you to eat."

Genesis 1:29 CEV

81

Volunteer your time:
Help out at an animal shelter
or at a homeless center.

Blessed is the one who is kind to the needy.

Proverbs 14:21 NIV

82

" True happiness comes from
the joy of deeds well done,
the zest of creating things new. "

Antoine de Saint-Exupery

Praise the LORD.
Praise God in His sanctuary;
praise Him in His mighty heavens.
Praise Him for His acts of power;
praise Him for His surpassing greatness.

Psalm 150:1-2 NIV

Pay a compliment:
Write an email
to someone,
thanking them
for a job well done,
or thank them
in person.

83

Imitate God, therefore, in everything you do,
because you are His dear children.

Ephesians 5:1 NLT

84

Get some animal
therapy: Spend time
with your dog or cat
and cherish their
undivided loyalty
and love.

The godly care for their animals.
Proverbs 12:10 NLT

85

" Tremendous happiness
and peace of mind are the
results of loving service
to others. Nobody can live fully
and happily who lives only
unto himself or herself. "

Gordon B. Hinckley

God has given each of you a gift from
His great variety of spiritual gifts.
Use them well to serve one another.

1 Peter 4:10 NLT

86

Use your gray matter:
Instead of watching TV,
why not try sudoku
or a crossword puzzle?

For the LORD gives wisdom; from His mouth
come knowledge and understanding.

Proverbs 2:6 NIV

Stop and smell the
roses. "Plenty of
people miss their
share of happiness,
not because they
never found it,
but because they
didn't stop to enjoy it."

William Feather

87

Let us come into His presence
with thanksgiving; let us make a joyful noise
to Him with songs of praise!
For the LORD is a great God,
and a great King above all gods.

Psalm 95:2-3 ESV

88 | Buy a journaling Bible and creatively journal your favorite verses.

May the words of my mouth
and the meditation of my heart be pleasing
to You, O Lord, my rock and my Redeemer.

Psalm 19:14 NLT

89

True happiness is complete
dependence upon God.

This is the day the LORD has made;
let us rejoice and be glad in it.

Psalm 118:24 ESV

90

Make iced tea
the old-fashioned way:
Boil up a fruit tea,
then add lemon, honey and ice.

Serve one another humbly in love.
Galatians 5:13 NIV

Hug someone:
"A hug delights and
warms and charms,
that must be why
God gave us arms."

91

If we love each other, God lives in us,
and His love is brought
to full expression in us.

1 John 4:12 NLT

92

Go for a walk in a
forest, on a mountain,
or on the beach.
Refresh your spirit
and use the time
to talk to God.

The LORD says, "I will refresh the weary
and satisfy the faint."

Jeremiah 31:25 NIV

93

Don't miss out on being
as happy as you can be:
Smile, even when
life gets you down.

O my Strength, to You I sing praises,
for You, O God, are my refuge,
the God who shows me unfailing love.

Psalm 59:17 NLT

94

Thank God for the blessing of today!

Give thanks to the LORD
and proclaim His greatness.
Let the whole world know
what He has done.

Psalm 105:1 NLT

Enjoy the
little things in life,
for one day you may
look back and
realize they were the
big things.

95

The hope of the righteous brings joy.
Proverbs 10:28 ESV

96

Live in the moment
and savor the now.
Focus on what is
around you and don't
be easily distracted.
Study your child's
drawing intently,
hug like you mean it
and feel the sunshine
on your face.

Teach us to realize the brevity of life,
so that we may grow in wisdom.

Psalm 90:12 NLT

97

Ditch the car.
Instead of driving to the store,
try cycling or walking.
You'll burn up some calories
and will be less likely
to buy unhealthy foods.

Do you not know that you are God's temple
and that God's Spirit dwells in you?
God's temple is holy,
and you are that temple.

1 Corinthians 3:16-17 ESV

98

Buy a pretty accessory to go
with an outfit, but remember:
A smile is the most stylish
thing you can wear.

Shout joyful praises to God, all the earth!
Sing about the glory of His name!
Tell the world how glorious He is.

Psalm 66:1-2 NLT

Don't worry.
Be happy!

99

Cast your burden on the LORD,
and He shall sustain you; He shall never
permit the righteous to be moved.

Psalm 55:22 NKJV

100 | Be a glass-half-full person.
Always look on the bright side;
it's good for you!

May our Lord Jesus Christ Himself
and God our Father, who loved us
and by His grace gave us eternal
encouragement and good hope,
encourage your hearts and strengthen you
in every good deed and word.

2 Thessalonians 2:16-17 NIV

101

Make a point of praying for the people who have upset or hurt you. Don't let bitterness and resentment steal your joy. Try to forgive and move on.

"Love your enemies!
Pray for those who persecute you!
In that way, you will be acting as true
children of your Father in heaven.
For He gives His sunlight to both the evil
and the good, and He sends rain
on the just and the unjust alike."

Matthew 5:44-45 NLT